Hard to Dance
with the
Devil
on Your Back

RAY BUCKLEY

Hard to Dance
with the
Devil
on Your Back

A Lenten Study for Adults

ABINGDON PRESS / Nashville

HARD TO DANCE WITH THE DEVIL ON YOUR BACK
A LENTEN STUDY FOR ADULTS

This book is printed on acid-free paper.

Library of Congress Cataloging-in-Publication Data

Buckley, Ray.
  Hard to dance with the Devil on your back : a Lenten study for adults
/ Ray Buckley.
     p.   cm.
  Includes bibliographical references and index.
  ISBN: 978-1-4267-1004-9 (book - pbk./trade pbk., adhesive - perfect
binding : alk. paper)   1. Lent—Prayers and devotions.   2. Lent—
Textbooks.   I. Title.
  BV85.B76   2010
  242'.34—dc22

                                                          2010038367

10 11 12 13 14 15 16 17 18 19 — 10 9 8 7 6 5 4 3 2 1

MANUFACTURED IN THE UNITED STATES OF AMERICA

*To Reverend Im Jung,
who followed the steps of St. John
through the desert and out again*

Contents

Hard to Dance
with the Devil
on Your Back

It seemed too early for a spring snow. This kind of heavy, wet snow usually came later. Walking up the street, the snowflakes stuck to my hat and coat as though they were determined to stay. Wet snow seems to have a purpose to it. The small smudge of ashes on my forehead was protected by my hat brim, and to be truthful, I had forgotten it was there. I was thinking about getting out of this Rocky Mountain snow and finding a warm place.

Not far in front of me was a man walking and twirling in the snow. His white rubber boots were pulled up over the bottoms of his pants. He was hatless. The snowflakes had stuck to his hair, weighing it down against his head. He was wearing his jacket inside-out, the yellow lining vivid against the worn, discolored red "cuffs." His gloves didn't match, but that didn't seem to bother him. As he passed me on the street, we smiled at each other, both fellow travelers. On his forehead, running gently toward his nose, was the same smudge of ash I wore on my own forehead. Ashes speaking to ashes.

Dance, then, wherever you may be . . .

There are times when *dancing* in the snow seems impossible because the drifts are too deep. Some who wear the ashes are praying for enough food or a safe place to sleep. Some have lost their life savings, and some fear for their lives. There are those who wear the ashes who have wronged others, and some who have mastered the art of appearance and forgotten how to *dance*. Some of us have been hurt so deeply that *dancing* again seems impossible. There are times when we have so institutionalized *The Dance* that we dance the same steps out of habit. There are times when we are so weary that we put on the ashes of Wednesday, just hoping, *Say something, God . . .*

On the wall of the Warsaw ghetto, a young Jew wrote, "I believe in the sun, even if it does not shine. I believe in love, even if I do not feel it. I believe in God, even if I do not see him." What enables faith to be transcendent and engaged even when events around us do not change? In every culture and time, persons of faith have surmounted, endured, and survived to "dance." They have danced with the weight of the world upon their shoulders. As Hans Küng would remind us, in the midst of it all we have been sustained by God, and that sustaining grace has enabled us to be helpful to those around us (*On Being a Christian* [Garden City, NY: Doubleday, 1976], p. 602). We dance while helping others dance.

Within some Native cultures is the tradition of circular story. This tradition uses story to contain truth and weaving story together to form a whole. The stories end when they come back to the beginning and have reached the end of the truth the storyteller wishes to share. These small studies are told in circular fashion, both individually and collectively. They begin and end with "The Dance." It is the way our lives are fashioned. Not the lines of individual lives marked along the way by events but woven together where story and event intersect—where God interacts and intervenes.

The season of Lent is a pilgrimage. It is not undertaken to give up a tiny portion of our excess as if it were a sacrifice but to exchange *our* way of seeing ourselves and the world for *God's*. It is to recognize the poor, our neighbor, and the alien differently. It is to wear the ashes and to know the Resurrection. It is to hope and to believe. It is to say with Jesus, "Nevertheless . . ." and know that no stone is too big to be moved.

The Dance

SCRIPTURE: Read 2 Corinthians 4:8-9; 2 Corinthians 12:9.

When I was a child, my family and I attended a church that did not encourage dancing. To be truthful, this church didn't encourage a lot of things. My father used to joke that at times some folks were so narrow-minded that if they hadn't had noses, their eyes would have bumped together. There were moments when it seemed that about all we could do for fun was to be hit by a bus and get prayed over for healing. (That, of course, is an exaggeration. A car would have worked equally well, particularly if the driver was going to see a movie.)

In our home we danced. We danced to music—spinning, jumping, and falling down. We danced in fun. We danced for the pleasure of dancing. Dancing is contagious with children. No one dances alone when children are present.

I remember the first time I heard Aretha Franklin sing. It was more than just music. It was as if there were things inside that you never knew were there until you heard her sing. It was as if all the things-you-had-wanted-to-say-and-couldn't-find-the-words-for were right there in her voice. It wasn't just feeling the music. It was experiencing the music, coming away a different person. Somehow, when the music stopped, the world seemed incredibly quiet. You wanted to play the song over and over and over to keep the feeling. You looked forward to the time when you could hear it again. Sometimes people thought you were crazy, playing the same song again and again . . .

I am not Aretha. I couldn't make those beautiful sounds. So I sang along with her.

In Scotland, when the English outlawed the playing of the great-pipes (bagpipes), Highland dancing, and the wearing of the tartan, people would go to church clutching small remnants of plaid between their thumbs and forefingers. When Irish clerics ruled that it was inciting immorality to move any part of your body in dance except your ankles and feet, the Irish began beautiful step-dancing, keeping the body rigid but moving the feet in intricate patterns and at varying speeds.

Among our Native people, dancing was a rich part of our cultures. There were social dances, times of community celebration, but there were also sacred dances. There was dancing that was prayer. In the late 1800s it became illegal to teach our children in our Native languages. The motto of one of the first boarding schools was "Kill the Indian, save the child." It became illegal to practice our ceremonies. Sacred things were destroyed or seized. Missionaries told us that our dancing was sin. When dancing is a form of prayer, and prayer becomes considered to be sin, then the spiritual core of a people begins to fragment. You begin to grasp for the sacred. At times you turn inward in despair, convinced that there is nothing good about the person God created.

In quiet places and in secret, some of the dancing continued, but some was lost for good. The lament in Psalm 137:1-4 became real:

> Alongside Babylon's rivers
>   we sat on the banks; we cried and cried,
>   remembering the good old days in Zion.
> Alongside the quaking aspens
>   we stacked our unplayed harps;
> That's where our captors demanded songs,
>   sarcastic and mocking:
>   "Sing us a happy Zion song!"
> Oh, how could we ever sing GOD's song
>   in this wasteland? (*THE MESSAGE*)

In Canton, South Dakota, there used to be the Canton Federal Indian Insane Asylum. Native people deemed insane were sent there for the rest of their lives. It was closed in 1934. In the investigation by the Bureau of Indian Affairs, which led to the institution's closure, it was determined that many of those incarcerated there had no form of mental illness. Some had received no medical examination, and no records were kept. Many had been traditional spiritual leaders who had refused to give up their religious beliefs, and because of that they were deemed insane, often through the influence of reservation missionaries. Nearly half of those held in the institution died there. There is a graveyard in Canton. It contains no markers and is in the middle of a golf course. These were the ones who literally refused to give up dancing.

The 2010 U.S. Census began in Noorvik, a small Native village in Alaska. As the first location for the census, media from around the world gathered to cover the first person registering for the census. It was the first time in almost one hundred years that Native dancing had been allowed in the village. Before then, missionaries had deemed it pagan, and it had long been illegal. Now, Native people from other villages came to teach them the old dances. The people of Noorvik had forgotten how to dance.

There are metaphors and similes so powerful that they can take your breath away. Imagine hearing the hymn "Lord of the Dance" when you haven't been allowed to dance. Imagine hearing of God dancing the world into being, God embodying the dance. Feel the weight of history, cultural and personal, when this line is sung: "It's hard to dance with the devil on your back." Yes. It is.

Here it is, laid out before us. Social, political, or other events may weigh us down in the dance, but the dancing is not gone, nor is the creative force that leads it. Dancing, after all, is not only a physical activity. It is an act of spirit and the Spirit.

It is hard to dance with the devil on your back. But it can be done.

In the play *The Great God Brown*, one of Eugene O'Neill's characters asks, "Why am I afraid to dance, I who love music and rhythm and grace and song and laughter?"

Following World War I, Germany was left in such depression and desperation (and kept there by world powers) that a wheelbarrow of

German currency would buy a loaf of bread. We are reminded by the German theologians of the early twentieth century that one may lose everything and know that God is enough. After having survived a concentration camp as punishment for hiding Jews during World War II, Corrie ten Boom shared the words spoken by her sister on her deathbed, "There is no pit so deep, that God's love is not deeper still." The noted psychiatrist and father of logotherapy, Viktor Frankl, after enduring the horrors of four Nazi concentration camps, would remind us that everything could be taken from you (your home, your family, your identity, even your clothing), but not your ability to choose how you will respond. That response is based on that which is deeply spiritual and meaningful. That can never be taken away.

Dance

The gospel is precisely about the dance. It is precisely about changing the concept of who can dance. It is about the right to dance. It is not all about the difficult times. It is also about the dance of joy. The dance of the spiritual life is real, and it is about discipleship that is real. It is about dancing when it looks like what you expected from life is crumbling. It is about dancing with burdens on your back, and still dancing. There is a Lord of the Dance and an inexplicable, inexhaustible invitation that is given to us. All of us.

The mind and spirit remember the dance long past the body's ability to produce it. You can "see" a dance even if you have no sight, and you can teach a dance even when you yourself can no longer dance. It is as if a phantom of the dance remains in the memory of our bodies.

Beautiful feet do not belong to dancers. It is human feet that dance, feet that must be coaxed at times to take the next step. Saints are beat-up, broken-down, and sometimes limping. Saints are also dancers. Dancing is not freedom from difficulties. It is faith in the middle of difficulties. For most Christians faith is not lived in abundance; it is lived in prayer. Discipleship is not an entrance into a safe world. Discipleship is a *shared* and *sharing* journey. In the dance, you are never alone.

Several years ago, I was in Nigeria. I had just arrived after nearly twenty-four hours of actual flying. It was pouring rain outside, and my luggage was thoroughly soaked. Even late at night, the traffic in Lagos seemed heavy. We arrived at the hotel where we would be staying for a night before heading inland. Even inside the room, you could hear the rain outside. I didn't really unpack. I just spread my clothes throughout the room to dry while I stumbled into a warm shower before going to bed. The flights had been exhausting.

Sometime in the middle of the night, I awoke to knocking on my door. I realized that it had taken me a while to recognize the sound, because the knocking became louder. Pulling on a shirt and trousers still damp from the rain and humidity, I opened the door to find two men standing in the hallway. One was our tall Dutch staff member in Lagos, and the other was a small African man. Both were drenched. "I know it's very late," the tall man said, "but would you mind if Eric shared your room tonight? He has come a very long way, and there is no place else."

Eric stood inside the door, carrying a small plastic bag and apologizing for disturbing me. I asked him if he would like to use the shower, and he nodded. I realized that he, like me, probably didn't have much of anything dry. I offered him my driest T-shirt, one that I usually wore when working. It was a 2X size. While Eric showered, I went back to bed, trying to stay awake at least long enough to say goodnight. It didn't happen.

Early in the morning, only a few hours later, I awoke to a sound. It wasn't offensive, certainly not loud, but different from what I was used to hearing. I ignored it and went back to sleep. But the sound continued, disturbing my sleep. Gradually I placed the sound as coming from Eric's bed. Finally I was awake enough to identify the sound as words—soft, rounded phrases, barely audible, but continual. Eric was praying, trying not to disturb me. He prayed for an hour. He prayed until I got up.

As we left the room that morning, Eric carefully wrapped the small pieces of soap from the bathroom in tissues and put them in his bag. I asked him if he would share some breakfast with me. Eric held my hand and prayed some more. We shared rolls and fruit.

For weeks, Eric had been walking, from a neighboring country. He was a refugee, carrying only a grocery bag. He had started his journey with a brother and had arrived alone.

Hard to dance

There is a story from Uganda during the time of Idi Amin. Christians would walk from their homes through the tall grass to pray in secret. As they walked, they would create a path through the grass. It was said that they could tell how their brothers and sisters were praying by the condition of their paths.

Sometimes we can tell how hard the dance is by the paths of those beside us.

It was Eric who taught me a valuable spiritual lesson: don't presume to judge how God is meeting the needs of others. How God sustains each of us in our life situations is not always open to interpretation by those looking in. This wasn't some lesson that I learned while observing him or conjecture on my part from having compared our two lives. He told me so, in almost those exact words. It was *his* country, *his* walk, *his* needs, *his* prayers, *his* brother.

Most of the world lives in poverty. Much of the world lives in political upheaval. We wear the same ashes of Wednesday. We arrive at the same Easter. And our prayers, the prayers of all of us, surround God like a mist. A plastic bag of clothes is not indicative of a failure on the part of God, the faith walk of one man, or the character of a people or country. It is a moment in history, a place on a journey. My heart broke, because I wanted Eric *to be like me*, which in reality, at that moment, meant having a couple of suitcases full of still-wet clothes. Eric asked me simply how he could pray for *me*. Need, uncloaked, meets grace.

I loved another deeply. I was not with her at the time of her death. After many years I have come to understand that I could have done nothing to prevent her death, nor to alter the circumstances of her death. For a time (a long time) I wondered why God had not been faithful to her in allowing her to die. Then I wondered if and how God had been faithful to her. We try to understand what is, to us, incomprehensible, because that is *our* need—to make sense of that which is beyond our imagination. It was *her* life and *her* moment of the death of *her* body. Was God faithful to her in life? Oh, yes. Was God faithful at the moment of death? Although I cannot touch it and cannot see it, I have come to believe it. There is a place of faith, both in the character of God and her own testimony (from an eyewitness account) that God's faithfulness to her was as personal as it always had been.

As followers of Jesus, we live in the real world. The real world hurts. Hurt, pain, illness, and crisis are not "where we want to live," but they are real. There's nothing spiritual about human suffering. There is, however, as Hans Küng tells us in *On Being a Christian*, a way to live, a way to dance, in the reality of suffering. Discipleship is not seeking (or glorifying) suffering. It is bearing suffering. Yet it is not simply bearing or enduring suffering; it is fighting suffering in our lives and in the world. It is not just fighting suffering but using suffering to change our lives and the lives of those around us. We are able to do this because we are sustained by God.

Frederick Buechner, in *The Magnificent Defeat*, penned:

> What we need to know of course, is not just that God exists, not just that beyond the steely brightness of the stars there is a cosmic intelligence of some kind that keeps the whole show going, but that there is a God right here in the thick of our day-to-day lives, who may not be writing messages about himself in the stars but in one way or another is trying to get messages through our blindness as we move around here knee-deep in the fragrant muck and misery and marvel of the world. It is not objective proof of God's existence that we want, but the experience of God's presence. That is the miracle we are really after, and that is also, I think, the miracle that we really get. ([San Francisco: Harper and Row, 1985], p. 47)

In her poem "Shooting Gallery," Luci Shaw describes some prayers as if we were in a carnival shooting gallery, shooting at tin targets, afraid that we might actually hit something and have to take home a prize. Then we see the feathers and smell the blood. The image is disturbing and poignant.

17

There is no dance without God and no dance in which God is not a partner. Everything that wounds us, wounds God; and every step we take in the dance, God takes with us.

Questions for Discussion and Reflection

1. How do we understand the faithfulness of God when situations seem impossible?

2. Is there a difference in how we expect God to be faithful to us in our culture and how we see God's faithfulness in other cultures or lives?

3. Victor Frankl speaks about our ability to choose our attitude in difficult situations. What is the role of God in helping us choose our attitudes?

4. What does it mean when we say that the gospel is precisely about changing the concept of who can dance?

5. Think about the story of Ugandan Christians and their prayer paths. How does your community of faith identify and support the needs of those within it?

6. In scriptures and in church traditions, we are accustomed to speaking of finding God's "presence." Does God as Person address our individual needs and situations? Explain your answer.

Prayer

Dance, O God.
Dance so that I can hear your footfall.
Dance before me,
So that I can follow.
Dance behind me,
So I know you have my back.
Dance beside me,
So that I may know you're with me.
Dance with me,
So that I may feel your heart.
Dance, O God,
So that I may know how. Amen.

A Parable

SCRIPTURE: Read Luke 12:32; Matthew 18:2-5.

The Lord of the Dance does not live within the walls that we create. These walls are often too restrictive for us, and they are not large enough for the Dance. Does not God dance in the streets, lifting those who cannot dance and inviting those who have not been asked?

A parable is a story used for teaching an idea. The gift of story is being able to encounter truth. All parables are truth. Some are also actual events.

There was a prosperous couple who attended their local church. Prosperity was not the problem. Their prosperity became a tool that they used to create influence and, from influence, power. The wife, as the Irish say, "fancied herself" a gifted pianist, and the husband "fancied himself" a man who made things happen, so a grand piano was given to the church, although it was much too large for the sanctuary. There were two brass plaques placed on the instrument: one on the piano itself and another on the beautiful adjustable bench. In a special service, the piano was dedicated to the glory and honor of God. It also came with the stipulation that the wife of the donor be the only person allowed to play the piano. Between services, it was locked with a key, and there were moments of righteous hysterics if someone had adjusted the bench to a new height during the week. On the rare occasion when the pianist was late, she would rush in and stand behind whoever was attempting to fill the vacancy, just waiting for the next stanza when she could occupy the adjustable bench.

In the same church was a father of three. He had a strong vocal presence in both the church and the community. He rarely missed Sunday morning worship service. Early in his marriage he had chosen to pursue other women, and what had begun casually became a habit. His wife and children endured the embarrassment of each situation, sitting with him Sunday after Sunday, and he without a thought in his mind of how his life affected those who loved him.

On a warm morning in late May, a middle-aged man, quite without the help of anyone in the congregation, found an unoccupied seat toward the back of this church and sat down. The congregation "passed the peace." He read the bulletin, and then the bulletin inside the bulletin. He found his way through the several forms of hymnbooks until it was time for congregational prayer. There were a host of "joys" as worshipers shared God's blessing in their lives. Then toward the end of the "concerns," as needs were being expressed, the man stood by himself, looking lost. His words defined the moment. "I'm not sure how to begin," he said almost too quickly. "My partner of thirty years died this week. We buried him yesterday, and I don't know how to go on. Could . . . would you pray for me?" He stood there for a moment, as if waiting for more words to come, and then he sat down. We all prayed as we did every Sunday morning.

It was one of those special Sundays where the men fixed an after-church breakfast. The men were good cooks and were known for cooking way too much bacon and sausage in proportion to the eggs. It was the enticement to stay instead of heading to the local restaurant. Nothing quite gets the post-Communion taste out of your mouth like pork products.

No one had invited the man who had visited that day. No one could really remember seeing him leave or when. At any rate, he hadn't been included in lunch, which was probably for the best because he was a topic of conversation. The loudest voices were those of the couple who had donated the piano and the father of three. The consensus of a few was that a meeting should be called before the following Sunday.

The next Sunday our guest was absent.

The following Sunday, our little pastor stood on a box behind the pulpit. Hers were the first words of the worship service. "I participated in a funeral yesterday," she began. "You'll remember the man who sat in the back a few Sundays ago and requested prayers for the loss of his partner." She paused. "This week he took his own life. In searching his belongings, his mother found our bulletin and thought maybe he was a member here. She asked if I would perform the funeral for him."

It's hard to dance . . .

That is the event as it happened. Here is the parable.

There once was a couple who had achieved a great deal in life. Inside it wasn't enough, so they used what resources they had to gain attention. They used a need within a community to create attention and dependence upon themselves with an instrument that was much too large. They used the instrument to create a sphere of influence and power and withheld those opportunities from others out of fear and a need to be recognized.

There was a church who dedicated an instrument to God's service knowing that what God is not free to control will never be a blessing. They were afraid there might not be another gift. Such is the danger of taking prayer requests from God's hands.

There was a man of influence in the community and the congregation who saw his desires as more important than his relationship with his spouse and children. What started out as a selfish risk became an indulgent habit. The shame of his wife and children, in a place designed for the lifting of shame, became routine.

There was a church who, because it was easier, did not confront the man in love and say, "There is much more to life for all of those involved. With God's help and the support of this community, life can be different."

There was a human being whose depth of grief and sadness brought him to the only place he knew to seek hope from God.

Who is the subject of the parable? It is all of us, for allowing a piano to stay, for allowing a brother to continue to abuse, and for allowing petty problems to keep us from seeing the soul God brought into our midst. It is all of us, for debating what we *thought* identified the problem, when the real problem was keeping a soul alive for one more week. We were given the opportunity to be God's people, but we debated the limits of how far we were willing to go as God's people.

Did we commit a great wrong? Several. At the very least, we weren't prepared to do right.

Sometimes the devil on our back is of our own making, and sometimes it is placed there by other people. Sometimes, we have never known what it is like to be without it.

Recently, I had a small role at a spiritual-formation event. It was actually a requirement that to teach, one needed to have been through the spiritual-formation process. I had not, but the organizers were kind enough to include me. During the course of the next few days, someone asked me why I had not been through the process. I was too embarrassed to say that I didn't have the financial resources to do so. Everyone at the event had the ability to pay several thousands of dollars over a period of a few years to be a part of these wonderful, life-changing events. Everyone had the time, the means, or the type of job that allowed them to be present to worship, study, and pray together. There was a reason that the poor and marginalized weren't present.

Several years ago, an event for children's ministry was held in a major city. It was held at one of the most exclusive hotels in the area, within walking distance of the city's attractions. The location was impeccable, the facilities beautiful and elegant. The hotel was surrounded on two sides by parks. Each morning the police department of the city would move the homeless off the sidewalks and to the other side of the park, so that those preparing for ministry with children would be safe. The last evening the event included a beautiful candlelight prayer walk to a river. Before the prayer walk began, the city moved the homeless.

In Anchorage, Alaska, the homeless began sleeping outside under the windows of a downtown church. One Sunday, the church members all brought rocks to put under the windows to keep them away.

Hard to dance with the devil on your back . . .

In the remarkable PBS series *Unnatural Causes: Is Inequality Making Us Sick?* one of the segments is titled "In Sickness and in Wealth." It examines the relationship between economic status and human health. The study began in Great Britain, then moved to Australia and the United States. It revealed some enlightening information. Even in countries with universal health care, economic class and social status are directly related to physical and mental health. There is an exact correlation between home ownership and healthy immune systems. We equate this with a sense of security in determining one's destiny. In short, our health depends in large part on our social status and resources.

What became clear to those conducting the study was that stress was one of the leading factors of poor health. Children from households where the parents rented had higher stress levels than children whose parents owned their homes. The stress factors of insecurity stemming from poverty result in poor health and a shorter lifespan.

Even with racial health tendencies figured into the quotient, the class distinctions remained. As wealth and social status declined, so did the quality of health. As security and social status increased, so did the quality of health. In the United States, the majority of the poor are white.

Here's the bottom line. In the whole world, power is health. Loss of power and social status affects our emotional, mental, and physical health. When financial security is lost due to worldwide recession or depression, when plants close or jobs are lost, we become more susceptible to stress.

Hard to dance with the devil on your back . . .

Hear the response of Jesus to messengers from John the Baptist, asking Jesus whether he is the One: the blind see, the lame walk, the lepers are cleansed, the deaf hear, the dead are raised, and the poor have received the good news. He did not say that the poor (the unincluded, pushed to the outside, unclean, poverty-stricken, no-account, and ne'er-do-well) have heard a sermon, but that the poor have the opportunity to be embraced by the gospel—wrapped up and bowled over in the love of God.

Jesus sits down with tax collectors and publicans, those who were thought unclean, and eats a meal (a sign of relationship). We are told that there were many of those considered unclean who followed Jesus and the disciples, and who *ate* with them.

Jesus sits down, and the children in the crowd gather around him. We look at the picture of Jesus with a kind expression on his face and beautiful, clean, combed children on his lap and around his feet. Jesus tells the disciples not to send the children away. Albert Nolan, in *Jesus Before Christianity,* speaks of the status of children in society in Jesus' time. Children had no status at all. A child was considered valueless. An unwanted child or a child of questioned lineage would often be left on the waste dump outside the city to die of exposure or be killed by animals. A child was considered disposable. Literally.

Jesus is saying to the disciples, "I want to give my attention and embrace to those who don't matter. The valueless are the kingdom of God." While the disciples are wondering what is happening, Jesus says, in essence, "Give up what you think you deserve and ought to have, and be like one of these." We are being asked to be childlike, to give up status, place, and value.

Here are the scribes whose education and learning gave them a position of prominence. Jesus says that it is those who have no education, the *napioi* ("infants" in Greek), who are the ones who really understand the message of hope.

As it turns out, we who have it all figured out—who have bloodlines, family identity, and student loans—are the needy ones. We're the ones who are having trouble dancing.

This isn't about being wealthy or being poor. It isn't about having positions of responsibility or being unemployed. We are told to rethink what we believe has value. We are told that blood is not thicker than water and that we are to have family-relationship with the unwanted. We are to give birthrights to those who have never known them. God is not asking us who we are but who we've adopted.

To the eunuchs who keep my sabbaths,
   who choose the things that please me
   and hold fast my covenant,
I will give, in my house and within my walls,
   a monument and a name
   better than sons and daughters;
I will give them an everlasting name
   that shall not be cut off. (Isaiah 56:4-5)

Isaiah speaks this promise of God to those whose bodies had been maimed and who, therefore, weren't allowed to worship in the temple. These are words of adoption to those who have not been able to dance. It is what enables those who have never even known the possibility of dance, to dance. And it is what enables a church in downtown Anchorage, Alaska, having placed rocks to keep the homeless away, to come back and remove the rocks they had put in place. And they did.

The dance is for people who do not matter. The Lord of the Dance is dancing with the worthless.

Questions for Discussion and Reflection

1. "The Lord of the Dance does not live within the walls that we create." What are the walls that we create as individuals and as institutions?

2. Who might be those who are on the outside of the Dance? In your community or culture, who are the "disposable" souls?

3. How have we experienced the outcast? What are our own experiences as outcasts?

4. Reflect on / discuss the thought, "In the whole world, power is health."

5. Is there a class structure within the community of faith? Is the ministry of the church structured for the inclusion of the poor or for ministry to the poor? Give reasons for your answers.

Prayer

Dancing seems impossible for some who have been wronged. As we prepare to overcome personal pain, we pray a simple prayer:

> Lord of the Dance,
> spit upon my eyes
> so that I can see.
> Change my focus,
> to see myself,
> and others,
> as You do. Amen.

For Further Reflection

Amazing Grace, DVD. Twentieth Century Fox, 2007.

The Wronged

SCRIPTURE: Read Isaiah 53:3; 1 John 13:34-35; Matthew 12:20.

My brother is about a decade older than I am. He is also my son. My brother is disabled, which doesn't mean much, except that he has different limitations than I do—and different gifts. Sometimes it takes him a while to understand something. Directions on labels are hard for him. Driving directions with landmarks are much easier. Reading is very difficult, but he likes to be read to. He is a champion of children, animals, the elderly, and the lonely. He laughs easily, and tears run down his face when he is very happy or deeply moved. He is excited when anyone receives an award, and he tells the whole town about any upcoming fireworks. It has taken me many years to get him to wear gloves when he is working, and now he makes everyone wear gloves.

Christmas at our house begins in October and ends in February. There is before-Christmas, Christmas and Epiphany, and after-Christmas. My brother doesn't believe in Advent. To him it makes no sense to pretend each year that Jesus hasn't already been born and to deny anyone the joy of singing Christmas carols all year long.

My brother is very world-wise. He has scars on his body that other people have placed there. He has been burnt with cigarettes and has had bones broken. I wish that I could have protected him before, the way that he protects me now.

My brother is my son.

My brother had historical status, but he had no legal status. For most of my life he has been my foster brother. He was always there whenever there was a need. He moved people from one house to the other. He painted walls when people needed help. He took people to the doctor and bought their groceries. He cooked when people were sick and shared what little money he had with anyone who needed it. He helped people decorate for Christmas because he wanted to, and he tried to find small presents for everyone he knew.

The truth is that sometimes his actions weren't good enough. For a small few on the inside and some looking in, it was as if he was not real. He was someone to whom every kindness was measured. He was someone who took away from the attention others thought belonged to them. I am sure that the wounds carried from childhood and the wounds inflicted by the callous still cause him pain. I am sure because I have seen the expressions on my brother's face.

There are those persons who spend their lives keeping others out. Give *some* people a key and they will go around locking every door. To some, a family name is deserved only by birthright. To some, affection is given in what amounts to a consolation prize. There are those who see the inheritance of family—love, inclusion, or material possessions—as being diffused when they are shared with others. A place at the table is shared grudgingly, and it is always viewed as an act of charity. The outsider has to measure up, be approved by the continually disapproving. The approval process never ends. We covet the appearance of sharing with the needy, but they dare not take our name or what we think belongs to us or our children. This is particularly true when how they think, feel, or appear might be a reflection on us. Few of us are willing to be "diminished." Except God.

Hear the words of Isaiah:

> He was despised and rejected by others;
>   a man of suffering and acquainted with infirmity;
> and as one from whom others hide their faces
>   he was despised, and we held him of no account. (53:3)

The nature of the gospel is such that when we wound another, we wound God. When we seek to protect our status, we cast away God.

A judge made my brother my son. A birthright. A right to birth. A place of belonging. Dance.

There are those people in our lives who remain cruel and distant no matter what we do. It seems as if the more we attempt to reach out, the more cruelly they respond. Many times they are within the circle of our own family. The wounds are not only open but are continually re-opened, and just when we think we can't be hurt any more, we are wounded again.

In Bette Greene's novel *Summer of My German Soldier,* a young twelve-year-old Jewish girl living in rural Arkansas at the end of World War II meets and befriends a German prisoner of war. Patty Bergen is the oldest daughter of a family that owns a dry goods store in a small town. Her father is detached, unloving, abusive, and tyrannical. While courteous to his younger daughter, he despises Patty. Patty's mother, Pearl, also favors the younger girl and publicly ridicules Patty for her looks, often in front of customers and visitors.

Near the end of the war, a German POW camp is built near town, and the first truckload of prisoners is sent to town to buy work hats. In the Bergens' store during that visit, Patty meets POW Anton Rieker. When he escapes from the camp, Patty finds him hiding in the attic of her parents' garage.

FBI agents and media pour into the little Arkansas town looking for the escaped prisoner. There have been few people in Patty's life who have cared for her, and in the person of Anton, who outwardly lives the opposite of her life, she finds someone who cares about her and who gives her hope. With Patty's help, Anton escapes to New York before being shot and killed. It is not until authorities question her that Patty realizes her "German soldier" is dead. In that moment, having lost friend and hope, Patty listens as her father berates and brutalizes her for defending a Nazi. In the end, Patty is sent to the Jasper E. Conrad Arkansas Reformatory for Girls.

There are many emotional moments in *Summer of My German Soldier*, many gems that sparkle; but there is one that stands out. The character of Ruth, the Bergens' African American housekeeper, brings wisdom, compassion, and nurturing to the lonely child. One day, when Patty is in despair over how she is treated by her parents, Ruth intervenes. She asks the child if she remembers the shirts that are marked "irregular" in her father's store. These shirts cost less because they are damaged. They are miswoven, sewn crooked, or missing buttons or buttonholes. They are not regular. They are irregular shirts.

Ruth reminds Patty that her father is like irregular merchandise. No matter how you love him, he will always be irregular. No matter what you try to do to make him love you, he will always be irregular.

Author Joyce Landorf Heatherley calls those difficult persons in our lives—the ones for whom we will never do anything right or say anything right— our "irregular people." If we allow them to do so, irregular people can keep us from dancing again or ever feeling as if we are worthy of the Dance. Irregular people tend to stay around.

Hard to dance with the devil on your back. Or in your living room.

On October 2, 2006, the Amish children at West Nickel Mines School in Pennsylvania had just finished playing outside for recess. They were settling back in to study in their one-room schoolhouse when Charles Carl Roberts IV backed up his pickup truck to the front door. At 10:25 a.m., he walked into the school. Releasing the boys and female adults, Roberts stood the female children against the blackboard. A little over thirty-five minutes later, Roberts shot the children and himself. Five Amish children died.

G. K. Chesterton wrote, "Fairy tales do not tell children that dragons exist. Children already know that dragons exist. Fairy tales tell children that dragons can be killed" (as quoted in Sabina Dosani and Peter Cross's *Raising Young Children: 52 Brilliant Little Ideas for Parenting Under 5s* [2007], p. 38). Monsters can live in the closet or under the bed. Dragons can be related to us or attend the same congregation. All of us, not just children, know that life challenges us with very real dangers and demands. We need to be reminded that we need not face dragons alone.

Do wounds feel different in Albania, Sierra Leone, or Michigan? Does the human spirit respond to pain differently in Afghanistan, Quebec, Dover, or Charleston? Darfur is not far removed from Dachau, except by time. Scars are scars. Is it true that what does not kill us makes us stronger? What is probably of greater truth is that what does not kill us forces us to live differently.

Can the church heal what the church wounds?

As second-, third-, fourth-, or tenth-generation Christians, some of our biggest spiritual battles will come from inside the church. Many of those who hurt us the most are part of the church. Within the church or the religious community, we often give ourselves permission to wound each other with sinful piety.

A story is told of a man and a church. For several years he attended church, sitting in the back of the congregation. He came in and out each Sunday. Some people were kind when they saw him there. Others stood apart with self-satisfied, saintly suspicion. It was easier to ask, "What do we really know about him?" casting just enough suspicion to keep him from being included. When he was ill, no one came to ask about him. When he was destitute, he was alone. Finally, he quit coming to church. And then the people said, "You know, he just doesn't bother to attend here anymore. He doesn't want to be involved." And after a while, this was said often enough that it came to be taken for truth.

People walk through the blood-red doors of our churches. If they are physically injured, we find them a place near an aisle. We locate a pillow to put under their injured limb, and we carry the Eucharist from the front of the church to where they are seated so that they may take part in Communion. We ask how they are healing, and we help them back through the red doors. What of those whose wounds are known (or unknown) but cannot be seen? Our churches are full of people who spiritually stagger from week to week, carrying wounds that would astound us if they could be seen. What of those whose wounds don't go away within a polite amount of time, or those who face dragons moment by moment?

Theologian Reinhold Niebuhr would remind us that institutions will always act in their own best interest, and the church is an institution.

Central United Methodist Church is celebrating its bicentennial as a congregation. The current building is located in downtown Detroit, Michigan. Detroit, with its beautiful architecture and rich history, has suffered such economic hardship that the exodus from the region is equated to the exodus from New Orleans after Hurricane Katrina. Neighborhood schools are being closed, and buildings and homes are boarded up. Detroit is in the process of reinventing, revaluing, and re-emerging.

Near Central Church is the stadium for the Detroit Tigers. New restaurants and venues have opened up, and the area has become a point of pride for the community. During events, parking becomes scarce as people flood into the surrounding blocks. Central Church is there, where it has been for so many years. On the street level of the building, the church has created an art gallery celebrating art that promotes peace. Neighborhood children can come in and create works of art.

On the cover of a recent issue of *Sports Illustrated*, there was a photo of Tiger Stadium and Central Church. The lines of people waiting to get into the stadium stretched across the picture. There was another line just as long in the photo. It was the line of people in need waiting to come into Central Church for food, clothing, counseling, and spiritual nurturing. Burdens are meant to be shared.

The Word of God for all of God's people

Dancing is not freedom from pain. We dance in spite of it. Pain is personal. It is carried day after day and sweated throughout the night. Pain, like poverty and poverty of spirit, is not abstract. It pushes through our psyches and expresses itself in how we breathe.

Suffering, even multigenerational suffering, calls us to live differently. It calls us to live differently when we witness and decide to share the suffering of others. It calls us to be hopeful and to extend hope.

After the shooting of the Amish children, the response of the Amish community was immediate. Within hours of the shooting, an Amish neighbor was at the home of the shooter, comforting his family. Roberts's father, so broken by what had happened, began sobbing uncontrollably. For almost an hour an Amish man held him in his arms while he wept. From around the Amish community, people visited the Roberts family and their extended family, bringing food and comfort.

At the funeral service of Charles Carl Roberts, thirty Amish came to support the family. In a community that often seeks privacy, the Amish invited Marie Roberts, the widow of the shooter, to attend the funeral of one of the children. "We must not think evil of this man," an Amish grandfather said.

It was in a letter addressed to the Amish community that Marie Roberts wrote, "Your love for our family has helped to provide the healing we so desperately need. Gifts you've given have touched our hearts in a way no words can describe. Your compassion has reached beyond our family, beyond our community, and is changing our world, and for this we sincerely thank you" (Damien McElroy, "Amish killer's widow thanks families of victims for forgiveness," *The Daily Telegraph*, October 17, 2006).

Scholars of Amish religious tradition remind us that for the Amish, the lack of vengeance does not undo the incredible wrong or exonerate the evil; instead it is the making of a conscious, deliberate step toward changing the future.

Forgiveness does not come from a place of moral superiority or "rightness." Forgiveness begins in the middle of pain. Its birth is visceral. It culminates in servanthood. Forgiveness may not mean a restored relationship, but forgiveness is relational. There is a maturing of forgiveness.

The forced removal of Cherokee, Choctaw, Chickasaw, Creek, and Seminole people from the American Southeast to Indian Territory (Oklahoma) took place over several years. Each tribe was removed from different locations and taken away by several routes. Many walked through the winter. At some junctures, families were split apart. Having been allowed only what they could carry or place in communal wagons, large numbers died of exhaustion, exposure, starvation, disease, and injury. Many Native Christian people carried pieces of their churches with them.

When the Choctaw arrived in what is now southeastern Oklahoma, they had almost nothing left. Many had died along the trail. News reached them of the Irish Potato Famine, and as the stories of starvation in Ireland and the plight of Irish immigrants were retold, the Choctaw pooled what little resources they had and sent it to the Irish to help them in their suffering.

Within a few days after the Pennsylvania shooting incident at the Amish school, the West Nickel Mine School had been torn down. In its place was left a grassy field with trees. Later a new school was built in a new location. Sometimes you need to dance in a new place. It is not necessary to go back to live in Babylon to heal from slavery.

Hear the words of Isaiah:

> He will feed his flock like a shepherd;
>   he will gather the lambs in his arms,
> and carry them in his bosom,
>   and gently lead the mother sheep. (40:11)

It is not an empty hope. In all times and in all situations we are sustained by God. When all seems hopeless, we are sustained by God. Unwanted, we are made family. Abandoned, we are adopted.

Questions for Discussion and Reflection

1. How do our own experiences of being wronged affect our spiritual journey?

2. Reflect on / discuss the question, "Can the church heal what the church wounds?"

3. What are some of the ways in which we are able to use the wrongs of our lives to help others?

4. Reflect on / discuss the following statements: "The nature of the gospel is such that when we wound another, we wound God. When we seek to protect our status, we cast away God."

5. Jesus spoke about forgiveness and addressed those who were unjust or self-righteous. How do we live in the presence of those who

continually do us wrong? How do we speak for those who are continually harmed?

6. Place yourself in the Amish community of West Nickel Mines following the tragedy that took place there. What of your faith would direct your choice of behavior in their situation?

Prayer

Lord of the Dance,
When there are no words,
You are the Word.
You are the Righter of Wrongs,
The Healer of Wounds,
The Listener of Cries,
The Possibility of the Impossible,
And the Lap on which we Rest.

Amen.

For Further Reflection

Donald Kraybill, Steven Nolt, and David L. Weaver-Zercher, *Amish Grace: How Forgiveness Transcended Tragedy*. Jossey-Bass, 2007.

Bette Green, *Summer of My German Soldier*. Puffin Press, 2006.

The Blind Side, DVD. Warner Home Video, 2010.

The Wrong

SCRIPTURE: Read Matthew 9:9-13.

The fifth step in the Alcoholics Anonymous program says, "Acknowledge to God, another human being, and myself the exact nature of my wrongdoing."

Imagine your life as a straight line or a linear plane. The beginning, as you know it, is your birth. Make a mark. That's a pretty important place to begin. Among the Yupik, indigenous people of Alaska, the English word for birth means "exit." Among some Native people, the word for birth means "to jump down." This is the place where you emerge.

On the line representing your journey, make a mark for each major event: your school completion, your first job, your choosing a partner for your life, your first pickup truck and dog to ride in the back. These are the events of our lives by which our culture measures our success. This is what makes us "us," the life to which our names are affixed. As if you were making a large *X*, make another line that crosses over yours. Make another; then another— as if you were emptying a box of wooden sticks into a pile on the floor. You know the game: move the sticks without disturbing the others.

Our lives are not a collection of events or achievements. Our lives are not even linear planes but rather intersections of relationships. Sometimes those relationships are for five minutes, sometimes for a lifetime. In the end, it is not about accumulation, credentials, or degrees. It is about how we responded to others. It is about how we responded to God.

When we are hurt or victimized, we see the pain on the "line" of our lives. We look for where God is acting on our "line." God *is* acting. God has jumped right smack in the middle of the sticks. God is acting in the lives of those who choose to cause pain and injustice. God is not a "just for me" God. God *is* for me. God speaks my language and my culture. God is seeking spiritual wholeness for all persons, the just and the unjust, even those who hurt us. God is seeking spiritual wholeness for us when we are the ones who hurt others.

It's hard to dance with a weight on our shoulders.

My father used to say, "Wrong people hurt too."

In the library of books that make up the Bible, Brother Mark remembered that many tax-collectors and "sinners" ate with Jesus and his disciples. There were many of them, and they followed Jesus (Mark 2:15). These were not the disciples but the breakers-of-the-law, the unclean, the soiled, the ones-we-have-to-be-cleansed-from. They followed Jesus, increasing in numbers, and ate with Jesus and the disciples. When you sit at a table with Jesus, you see yourself clearly. Kept away from the table, you see only your denial.

In the language of the church, we speak of a "common table," a shared Eucharist or a place of inclusion for the diversity of the Body of Christ. The "common table" was never intended to be owned by the church. It is not just the opening of the church walls but the breaking of the walls. It's the place where anyone can just walk in the door, as good as you please, and sit down.

Children's books often have great treasure for adults. We grow into children's literature and find richer meaning with the years. Shel Silverstein's *The Giving Tree* is such a book.

In *The Giving Tree*, a small boy and a tree have a relationship. The boy climbs the tree, rests in her shade, eats her apples, and loves her very much. The story tells us that the tree was happy. As the boy grows older, he leaves the tree alone more often. He returns and asks the tree for money. The tree has no money but offers her apples. In each subsequent encounter, the boy-turned-man asks the tree for something he wants. The tree instead gives of herself: her branches to build a house, her trunk to build a ship to gather wealth. Each time she gives, the story remarks,

"And the tree was happy." But after each gift the man does not return until he needs something else. Finally, old and bent, the man returns to sit and rest on all that is left of the tree—her stump. And the tree was happy.

The dichotomy of the story is profound. This tree, who loves this boy, continually gives herself away. The boy loved the tree when the greatest joy of his life was to be in her presence. The boy-man becomes a taker, a user, an opportunist who sees the tree for what he can gain from her, giving nothing and taking everything. When old and alone, he sits on all that is left of the tree. And the tree is happy? Yes, because the boy is back. My God. Yes, my God.

Dance.

There is a true Native story that is part of Plains oral history. When a young man wished to marry a young woman, he would bring gifts to her family. If he was fortunate enough, he would bring horses. Sometimes he would be required to bring many horses. It was not a bride purchase but a way of showing honor and his ability to provide.

An older chief had a beautiful younger wife whom he loved very much. As time passed, she fell in love with a younger man, and the couple fled the community amidst dishonor and fear. After a time, the older husband sought out the young couple, bringing with him many horses. He gave the horses as a gift and left the couple in peace. He had also given them a way to return.

There are moments when the wrong is so unthinkable, so beyond humanity and heaven, that the love of God seems unjust. The love of God is not passive; it is fierce in its purpose and intensity. The love of God illuminates for us who we are and what we are capable of becoming. We stand exposed, not to God but to ourselves. God has known us all along.

Some years ago I was part of a group of people sitting behind closed doors to listen to and enable the telling of stories. The majority of the people in the room were elderly Korean women. During World War II, they had been known as "comfort women."

The mass rape and sexual slavery of women during World War II is almost unfathomable. As early as 1932, prior to the Sino-Japanese War, women across Asia, as well as girls as young as thirteen, were kidnapped and forced into organized "comfort houses," where they were raped by as many as fifty soldiers a day. The vast majority were from Korea, but there were also some Dutch, some Chinese, and some from other small Asian countries. They were given minimal food, beaten, and forced to endure abortions without pain medication. They were injected with sterilizing drugs. Their names were forgotten, and the records of the comfort houses were destroyed. The actual number of rapes may have been close to ten million.

As the war reached a conclusion, most of the comfort women were executed or simply left to die. Nearly all of the comfort women died without their stories ever being told. Those who survived not only suffered irreversible physical and mental trauma, but they were unable to tell their stories because of personal and cultural shame.

By sheer numbers, the unorganized rape and abuse of women by Russian troops exceeds that of Asia. In the final days of World War II, German, Polish, and Russian women were routinely raped by Russian soldiers.

An elderly Korean woman, Grandma Kim Hak Soon, told her story in 1991. She was the first.

Behind the closed doors, the room was quiet. People greeted one another with respect and found their seats. In this place, there was no official agenda or moderator, just awareness that starting might be difficult. The sacredness of personal story is profound. Personal story is not always meant to be shared except in a safe setting, and those are rare. In this room, the weight of stories and the years of silence were palpable. How does one begin the first words of what was held secret for so long?

Some women could not speak. Instead, they had brought drawings and paintings—imagery instead of words. People wept openly and quietly. In some cultures, painful stories are hard to recount for fear that the speaking aloud will give them rebirth. The stories that day stayed inside the walls, where they were meant to be.

Time had passed. In a meeting in northern California, an elderly Korean woman accompanied by younger members of her family greeted me. Years before, I had seen one of her paintings and listened to her story. As we spoke quietly through the translation of her family, her grandnephew said, "She answers letters." For a moment I thought that he was asking me to write to her. He said, "She receives letters from people in Japan, and she writes back."

When she was able to speak her story, she received a letter from a person in Japan apologizing for the great hurt in her life. She answered in the same spirit, offering consolation. There arrived another letter from a different person, followed by another. Her name was being shared. And to each one, she wrote words of peace. The years had been spent quietly writing letters.

I asked how she could do this. Her answer was, "Because I am able."

Dance as you are able. Dance as God enables you. We cannot undo our wrongs or the wrongs of others, but we can do what God enables us to do. We can open up the corners of our soul to the Spirit of God, speak the truth, do justice, and seek healing relationship.

In 1864, Territorial Governor John Evans of Colorado authorized the forming of a militia to "kill Indians." To lead the militia, he chose John Chivington, a former presiding elder of the Rocky Mountain District (1860, 1861) of the Methodist Episcopal Church. Evans and Chivington had begun the Denver Seminary, a Methodist Seminary. On July 22, 1863, the "First Methodist Episcopal Church of Denver" was incorporated, with John Evans and John Chivington listed as two of the five trustees.

On November 28, 1864, John Chivington led a group of Colorado troops into a camp of peaceful Cheyenne and Arapahoe. Women and children huddled into groups, where they were shot. Babies were taken from the arms of dying mothers and shot. The name *Sand Creek* echoed around the world. Chivington, who earlier had advocated the killing and scalping of Indian children, was quoted before the raid as saying, "Damn any man who sympathizes with Indians. . . . I have come to kill Indians, and believe it is right and honorable to use any means under God's heaven to kill Indians." Chivington led his men through the streets of Denver, some wearing the body parts of men, women, and children killed at Sand Creek. On the steps of a church, speeches were given in Chivington's honor.

In the aftermath, John Evans was removed from his post as governor, and John Chivington was removed from his leadership of the militia. A few years later, he was preaching again, still convinced of his "rightness."

It is hard to dance. It is hard to imagine.

JuDee Anderson is a member of Sheridan United Methodist Church in Sheridan, Wyoming. A therapist, she had heard the history of Sand Creek while working there, and she now worked on the Northern Cheyenne

Reservation. As she shared the story of the Sand Creek Massacre at her church, the people in Sheridan asked how they might be involved. Descendents of the victims of the massacre spent hours patiently sharing their history and their present. Members of the church went to the Northern Cheyenne Reservation to listen and learn. Cheyenne tribal members asked to come to the church, and together they sat at a meal. Each journeyed to the "home" of the other. The church and the Northern Cheyenne descendents of the Sand Creek Massacre ministered to each other.

Every spring, following the path of John Chivington to Sand Creek, an annual spiritual healing run is held to heal the earth and the people. JuDee and the people of Sheridan UMC asked, "What can we do?" The answer was simple. There was a need to take buffalo meat to the site. They did it. When the site of the Sand Creek Massacre was dedicated, church members were present. When human remains of the Cheyenne and Arapahoe were returned and reburied, church members were there, sharing in the grief and the homecoming. Together, they struggled with finding enough financial resources to help with needs as they arose. Sometimes there were major roadblocks. More important, they began to search out healing and recovery for historical trauma, and they became family. JuDee says it simply, "Together, we're working to bring healing. For us, it is not just about listening and learning. It is about finding the truth and taking the responsibility. It is about owning the truth."

The Word of God for the people of God. Thanks be to God.

There is yet no resolution for the "comfort women," nor for the Northern Cheyenne, Southern Cheyenne, Northern Arapahoe, or Southern Arapahoe. They still find it difficult to speak of the tragedies of generations ago. How is the gospel, the good news, spoken to every people and nation around the globe when all have known genocide, war, tyranny, slavery, and trauma?

There is a difference between God and the church. God works in the world through God's people—the church but not only the church. The church is a voice for God, but it is not God's voice. There are whole populations across the globe who cannot dance because they have been taught to believe that their cultures and ethnicities are inferior to others, and they have never danced without the weight of inferiority on their back. That is often what the church has brought. In the United States,

Prohibition was as much a reaction to Irish, German, and eastern European immigrants as it was an opposition to alcohol.

When we seek power in or outside of church and attempt to assert our will instead of seeking the will of God, we do violence to God. When we speak of the "right" of the church, we are obligated by the gospel to speak of "the wrong." When we speak of the wrong, we are compelled to look at ourselves. When we look at ourselves, we are met by God.

Recently, the United Church of Christ produced a television commercial whose final culminating thought was, "God is still speaking." Yes. God still has God's voice.

There is no justification to human suffering, no understanding it. There is no spiritual glory in equating the suffering of the world with the suffering of Jesus. Jesus spoke hope in God in the middle of suffering.

Hear the words of Jesus in Brother Matthew's book:

> Blessed are the poor in spirit . . .
> Blessed are those who mourn . . .
> Blessed are the meek . . .
> Blessed are those who hunger and thirst for righteousness . . .
> Blessed are the merciful . . .
> Blessed are the pure in heart . . .
> Blessed are the peacemakers . . .
> Blessed are those who are persecuted for righteousness' sake . . .
> Blessed are you when people revile you and persecute you . . .
>   (Matthew 5:3-11)

In some inexplicable way, it is often those we hurt who lead us back to the dance. It is through those we have wounded that we find our way home.

Questions for Discussion and Reflection

1. Does God measure wrong? Does God measure right? Give reasons for your answers.

2. Think about the idea that "wrong people hurt too." Is there a point where the gospel ceases to address the depth of wrong or the extent of wrongdoing? Explain your answer.

3. What is the role of justice in the lives of the unjust?

4. Rethink the story of *The Giving Tree* by placing yourself in the position of the tree. What are your thoughts and feelings from this perspective? Have you been in the position of the boy/man in the story?

5. The horrors of the tale of "comfort women" and the event at Sand Creek are profound. Where do they take us as God's people?

6. What is meant by the phrase, "There is a difference between God and the church"? Does God speak only through those who know God? Explain your answer.

Prayer

Lord of the Dance,
search me.
Know my heart.
Help me to know my heart.
Keep me close to yours.
O God, my God,
Bring me home. Amen.

For Further Reflection

Shel Silverstein, *The Giving Tree*. Harper & Row, 1964.

Brown, Dee. *Bury My Heart at Wounded Knee: An Indian History of the American West*. Holt Paperbacks, 2007.

Yoshiaki Yoshimi, *Comfort Women*. Columbia University Press, 2002; Suzanne O'Brien, translator.

The Disciple Whom Jesus Loved: Judas

SCRIPTURE: Read John 13:21-30; 1 John 4:18.

It was a gathering of intimates, friends of sorts, for a meal that occurred each year. The smell of food filled the space. Wine was poured into cups and spilled casually on the table. Perhaps only one person present knew how events would soon rapidly change the lives of those in the room. There was one other who knew something about these plans, but he didn't really have a clue as to their impact. This group had come together to share a meal. It was Passover, a meal that today begins with the question, "Why is this night different from all the others?"

Sometime during the meal Jesus' heart is breaking, so much so that his distress is visible to those sitting around him. The accounts that we have are very simple. He says, "One of you is going to betray me."

It's out. Nothing about the meal will ever be ordinary. The food, the wine—none of it matters. "One of you is going to betray me."

It is in the book that John wrote (tradition tells us that he is describing himself as the disciple "whom Jesus loved") that we hear Peter ask John to find out of whom Jesus is speaking. John, who is reclining against Jesus with his head on his shoulder, asks, "Who is it?" Jesus says, "It is the one to whom I give this piece of bread dipped in the cup."

The hand of Jesus places the gift into the hand of Judas, and the voice of Jesus says, essentially, "Go on. Let's get it over with."

Eugene Peterson, in his epic work *The Message*, says simply, "Judas, with the piece of bread, left." Judas left, carrying the sodden bread with him. The day was ended. The night was upon them.

I arrived in Boston to go to college. I had been on one long plane trip before, but I had never flown to a place where I would stay. I've often imagined that there weren't many others that year whose luggage contained a fringed deerskin jacket and a pair of elk-skin moccasins.

One of my first friends was from New York City. He introduced me to a world that I had never seen before. From him I learned to ride the Red Line from Quincy to Cambridge. I learned to be a better student and a lifetime student. From him I learned, and am still learning, to be a better human being.

On a late autumn day we rode the Amtrak from Boston to New York, got off at Grand Central Station, and caught the subway almost to his home. There had been so much to see, so much that was new, that until we arrived at his house nothing was familiar. When we walked through the door, there was the warmth that came from an oven that had been at work all day. The moist air hung around our heads, infused with the smell of bread. Suitcases were left in the hallway; coats were hung on the stairwell as we were ushered to a table and sat down shoulder-to-shoulder. A blessing was said over the meal. I didn't understand the language, but I knew the spirit of the words. A loaf of bread, the gift of a day's efforts, was broken. Levi's father stood, dipped the bread in salt, and handed it to me to eat. A glass of wine was poured for me. I looked at my friend. He smiled and nodded. Everyone around the table smiled and nodded. I ate the bread and took a sip of wine. I was the honored guest.

Some years later, the three of us had a conversation, one of many that changed me. "Sometimes you Christians miss an important portion of the story of the Last Supper," Levi's father said, leaning forward in his chair. "Judas is the honored guest. By his action, Jesus is telling Judas, 'At this moment you are the closest to my heart. You are loved.'"

"How can that be?" I asked, pretty sure that there must have been some misunderstanding. "Jesus said that it would have been better if Judas had not been born" (see Mark 14:21).

"Yes. Could it be that Jesus knows the events of the life of Judas and how Judas would be remembered?" he said. "If the account of John the Apostle is correct, then what Jesus did *culturally* was to tell the disciples and Judas, *by action*, that Judas was loved, and perhaps the most loved at that moment. It was *his action* that made the difference."

There is a room on the second story. It is spacious and clean. Peter and John have secured it on the instructions of Jesus and made preparations for the Passover meal. Jesus is aware that this will be the final meal with his disciples before his death.

Hard to dance . . .

In reality, Judas has already betrayed Jesus. It really is only a matter of a kiss away. He comes to the Passover meal and climbs the stairs.

Hard to dance . . .

The other gospels tell us of the bread and wine that would become the Eucharist. It is the testimony of John that tells us the story of one piece of bread dipped into wine and passed from hand to hand. We don't know when it occurred during the meal. It is a night of the unexpected. The disciples argue among themselves as to which one will be the most important. While Jesus is preparing for betrayal, the disciples are planning their future.

Jesus tells the disciples that one of them will betray him. The anxiety of the moment is tearing his heart. During the course of the meal, the disciple "whom Jesus loved" had eaten next to him, reclining and resting his head on the shoulder of Jesus. Desperately, Peter beckons to him, saying, in essence, "Find out; who?"

The act of breaking the bread and dipping it is an act of love. Jesus dips the bread and hands it to Judas. The incompatibility of betrayal and love must have been palpable. Jesus identifies the betrayal, bringing the issue into the open. He identifies what his action will be. (How that must have confused the disciples.) In a room full of people who love him and whom he loves in return, he breaks the bread, dips it, and places it into the hand of Judas. This bread, marked as the body of Christ. This wine, identified as the blood of the Crucified. Hand touching hand. Wine staining both.

There is one with whom I have eaten every day who will betray me. (Some of you will deny me.)

I know the identity of this person. (I am aware of your weaknesses.)

He will identify me with a kiss. (I will identify him with an act of love.)

I will place what identifies my life into this person's hands. (What he seeks to take, I will give.)

Betrayal is often so soul-wrenching that exposure becomes a reward in itself. Judas fled, not because of exposure but because of the gift. In his hand he carried a wet piece of bread whose stain would stay with him for the few remaining days of his life. Had he eaten it, would the story be different? Jesus would still have been held captive and crucified. But what of Judas? Here's the hopeful part of the story: he took the bread with him.

Matthew is the only gospel that tells of Judas after his betrayal of Jesus. Matthew tells us that the sun had just risen when Judas entered the temple. He tried to give back the thirty pieces of silver he had received for betraying Jesus. There were two things he knew: he had sinned, and he had betrayed an innocent man. The morning after Peter denied Jesus three times and spent the night in agonized weeping, Judas hanged himself (see Matthew 27:1-5).

In the traditions of some cultures around the world, the death of Judas was the understandable response for one to take after betraying another and causing that person's death. Unable to change what had been done, Judas threw the money back. Unable to move forward through the shame, and unable to go back, he killed himself. He did not know, nor did the disciples, that in a few hours the rules would all be changed.

How many times have we walked up the stairs into that room, thinking that no one knows what is happening to us or because of us at that very moment?

It's hard to dance . . .

It's not that I'm the only one; after all, there are those sitting around the table planning their advancement in the group. After all, Jesus called Peter by name. It may not even be a matter of life and death. It may not amount to anything. Maybe it won't be so bad tomorrow. There is this weight upon my spirit. How long has it been there?

It's so hard to dance . . .

Then everyone is looking at me. No one has spoken my name, but everyone knows. Yeah, you're not so perfect, Mr. Peter Gonna-deny-him-three-times! Just let one of them bring it up!

Then, there it is, dripping from the hand of Jesus onto the table. This doesn't make sense. He knows. Everyone in the room knows, and he is showing, by this piece of bread, that I'm the loved one here. Surely he's mocking me! But he's made the commitment. There is no mockery in this sacred act.

It's hard to dance. It's hard to breathe.

Wordlessly, I take the bread. I take the bread. In my hand I carry it, knowing what a priceless gift it is, and it drips between my fingers. But I don't let go as I go into the night.

From the beginning, there was nothing secret to Jesus about the plans of Judas. Yet Judas was loved anyway. Before he betrayed Jesus and repented, he was forgiven. Before he kissed Jesus, he was given the token of God's love. Before Judas could do anything, God's preparations were already there.

There is a saying from the French, *"L'amour de Dieu est folie"*: "The love of God is folly." The love of God is so much greater than we can imagine, so breaking-of-the-laws, so breaking-of-the-rules, so beyond our acts of betrayal—our kisses and stained fingers—so impossible that it seems like foolishness. "My God," we say casually, not realizing that God *is* ours.

The book of Hosea is a love story. It is profound because it seems impossible, certainly improbable. It is a love that breaks the rules, denies reason, and violates self-protection.

The story begins with God. God tells the prophet Hosea to marry a prostitute. He is told to marry someone who God knows will not be faithful. God surely knows that this will break the heart of Hosea. God tells Hosea to conceive children with Gomer, his wife. The children were named Jezreel, No-mercy, and Nobody. Every day Hosea, Jezreel, No-Mercy, and Nobody walk through the streets, Hosea trying to preach to the people around him. But they know his wife. They know where she is.

When Gomer's beauty has faded and all the spent years have accumulated, she is put up for sale. God says, "Hosea, love her again. Start all over again, take her home from the brothels, and love her as your wife." Hosea's heart was breaking.

Hosea says, simply, "I will." Hosea went and bargained for his wife. He paid the price one would pay for a fine slave. And he loved her.

There is a part two to the story. It is the story of God and Israel, a nation who had turned its back on the love of God for what was a more fashionable, less relational faith. Hear the words of God, "Israel, How could I give you up? My very heart turns at the thought of it. When you were a child, I loved you, and it was I who taught you how to walk. I held you in my arms, but you had no idea that I was looking after you. I was like someone who picks a baby up and holds its face against my cheek. Do you remember?"

The lesson of Hosea became the act in the upper room. "I know of your betrayals. I was there. I know of the laughter. I felt it cut into me. I know of the law and of the self-righteous. I have another plan. Let's go home. I will pay whatever price I have to. They may not understand the price and think I am foolish (*l'amour de Dieu est folie*), but isn't foolishness an abandoning to love? I'm the Lord of the Dance. And I can change the rules."

Here it is, in the moment in front of us. God knows us. God sees in those places of our hearts where no one else sees. God sees those devils upon our back that have kept us from dancing, sometimes for fear of what others may know and for fear that we won't be allowed in. God says, "It has broken my heart, and it has broken yours. How can I give you up?" And God holds something out with sticky fingers and places it into your hands. This time, you take and eat it, and get back up to dance again.

Questions for Discussion and Reflection

1. Reflect on / discuss the meaning of the statement "mercy is not a feel-good experience."

2. Jesus clearly has not just an *awareness* of the betrayal of Judas but he also deeply *feels* the betrayal. How does one extend the cup while hurting? How does one respond, knowing that the wrong has yet to occur but is certain to occur?

3. Why do you think Judas carried the "sop"—the wine-soaked bread—with him into the night?

4. Think about the statement "the love of God is folly." What does that statement mean to you? What might it say about the love of the church?

5. How does the story of Jesus and Judas compare to the story of Hosea and Gomer?

Prayer

> Lord of the Dance,
> My God, my God, my God.
> The bread has stained my fingers.
> Your touch has stained my heart.
> I cannot wash them off.
> They are not wine, but love.
> I'm tired of running out into the night.
> Let me dance again. Amen.

When Worlds Collide

SCRIPTURE: Read Jeremiah 18:1-6; Isaiah 49:16.

D r. C. Everett Koop, former Surgeon General of the United States, wrote a very small, simple story about the death of his son, entitled *Sometimes Mountains Move* (Carol Stream, Ill.: Tyndale House Publishers, 1979). An expert mountain climber, Dr. Koop's young son was tragically killed in a climbing accident. His death was unexplainable. He was skilled and proficient. The equipment was excellent, and the climb itself was executed well. The investigation could find no error, nothing to which his death could be attributed. Nothing could be explained. Then the rarest of occurrences was discovered: the mountain had moved. The precipice of rock had moved a fraction, but it was enough to cause the death of a young climber who had done everything correctly.

Sometimes mountains move. When we have made the best of plans, and have done what was needed, mountains still move. The unexplainable happens.

I was in St. Louis in the middle of summer, and outside it was hot and humid. The air-conditioning in the hotel made everything comfortable, and you could look out the window and see the sun without experiencing the heat. That probably would have been my preference, but two things had happened: the little bit of money that I had brought had been stolen, along with my wallet, and the colleague who would bring replacements for me would not arrive until the next day. There were three one-dollar bills in my pocket.

Just up the street from the hotel was a Wendy's restaurant, and I knew that it was about the only place these few dollars might stretch. On one side of the restaurant was a group of tourists. The other side was empty except for one large man. His clothes and hair were dirty. He had been out in the heat all day, probably for several days. He was simply sitting at a table, staring down at it, shaking the ice in his cup.

I found a small table not far from him, the two of us sitting on the same side of the restaurant, and I started to eat, just looking at my food. "I used to be somebody," he said. A few people looked at him. "I used to be somebody," he said again. I kept on eating, not really sure what to do. "I used to be somebody," he said loudly, standing up. This time everyone looked at him, and then looked at me to see what I was going to do. I looked at him, and he walked over and sat down in the yellow chair across from me.

His story unfolded quickly, word by word—the life that used to be and the pictures of people with whom he had once had a relationship. I left the food on my tray, making eye contact. If I looked away, he searched my face until he found my eyes. Before he had finished his last few sentences, he was moving for the door, and then he was gone.

I was not able to eat, nor was I able to throw away the food on my tray. It was left there on the little table. I went after him, but he had gone. *I used to be somebody.*

If my money had not been stolen, I would have been eating in a hotel. The heat would have kept me inside where I could look out without going out. I was not there for him. He was there for me. The *somebody* I used to be was different.

I have loved you with an everlasting love . . . (Jeremiah 31:3)

In the Canadian far north, the Inuit have a tradition of creating *inuksuit* (plural). An *inooksuk* (singular) is a creation of stones from the tundra. Using stackable rock and long, flat stone, an image is created that is roughly that of a human being. In this region of the world, through ice and snow and the short melting of summer, an *inooksuk* may remain in place for a thousand years. Like other historical wanderers around the globe, the Inuit, by making *inuksuit*, leave a message for those who follow after. It may be the place of a good camp. It may be a place where animals gave themselves to hunters to sustain the people. It is a reminder in stone, the shape of a human being, that something of significance happened to human beings in this place.

Job is a marker of human experience. Job experiences the loss of family, health, acquisitions, and security—and, in a real sense, friends. Job is a person who has done it right, who has lived right. The experience of Job does not make sense. He yells at God, and he asks the question, "Why me?" In the middle of losing everything, God gives Job no answer, and the answers Job receives from the know-it-alls around him are an insult. Through the experience of Job we are made aware that good outcomes do not always come from good living. In fact, the opposite sometimes seems true. Faithfulness to God is sometimes followed by the same disappointment and devastation as those who make no acknowledgment of God.

In Jeremiah 18, the prophet is instructed by God to go down to the house of the potter. There the artist is making a clay vessel on a potter's wheel. With the hands of the potter molding and shaping the clay, the vessel is damaged and destroyed. The potter picks up the remains of the vessel-in-the-making, shaping it into a ball of clay and removing the trapped air. Placing the clay in the center of the wheel, the hands of the potter begin to shape it again into something useful.

The message of God is very simple: *I want to do this for you, O Israel.*

There have been so many beautiful songs written, and so many powerful sermons preached, about broken vessels. The images are beautiful and meaningful. God picks up the fragments of the broken vessels and puts them back together again. But God is showing Jeremiah something entirely different. The vessel is not fired; it is in the process of being shaped in the hands of the potter. It is not broken by winds or rain; the form of the clay is destroyed with the potter's hands still around it. Pieces are not glued back together again. The potter creates a new vessel that is appropriate for the potter's purposes. God is not saying, "Let me repair you." God is saying, "Let me make you into something new."

After a painful time in my life, my father came to my home. He was wearing his tattered jean jacket and his cowboy hat from the Montana State Fair. He had worn the hat for so many years, through all kinds of weather, that its brim no longer turned up. He also had a Stetson that Mom had given him, but he wore this old one when it didn't matter what happened to his hat.

In my father's hand was a small, blank book. Inside the cover, in his handwriting, was the text from Jeremiah 18. Just below it was written, "Sometimes lives are damaged in the hands of the Potter." The book was a prayer journal of sorts. Really, it was a forgiveness journal. In it, I was to record events and begin to pray for those involved. As God enabled me to forgive, I was to write the date in red by the name, so that one day I would be able to look back and see the new vessel God had made of me.

Sometimes lives are damaged with both hands of God around them. We have not failed God. We have not somehow failed in our faith journey. God has not deserted us. We are clay. We are broken while still in the hands of the Potter.

Cancer came into my life and then went into remission and seemed to go away. A few years later, cancer returned in a different form. In the small church that my brother and I attended, there were several people with cancer, most of them young parents. One Sunday morning at the close of the morning worship service, our church gathered around us, each person placing their hands on those around them, linking the congregation, the pastor, and those of us kneeling at the front. My brother was certain that the cancer would disappear, but it had not. It would disappear for me after a time, but not for all of us who were kneeling at the front of the church. I was struggling with a way to talk about the illness with him.

It was near Christmas, and where I worked, each staff member was given a Christmas ornament: a small, hand-blown glass bird in a beautiful gold box. When I opened mine, I discovered that one of the wings was broken on the ornament. As I sat and looked at it, the image became more real and the significance became clear.

Nearly every Christmas, I write my brother a short story. That evening, after he went to sleep, I sat up and began to write the tale of a small bird. She could fly beautifully, and she was known as She Who Flies Swiftly. One day she is found beneath a tree, having broken her wing. The Creator, walking through the forest, picks her up, touches the broken wing, and lays her back down. Each day, she expects to fly, having been touched by the Creator, but she cannot. She calls after the Creator, day by day, not realizing that her cries have become song. Then, for a moment, the Creator sings with her. The broken wing remains broken, but her song becomes permanent. Her name is changed from She Who Flies Swiftly to She Who Has Been Healed.

God always brings healing, but the circumstances of our lives are not always changed. Sometimes we are not cured. We may walk carrying plastic bags. We may endure war, poverty, persecution, and disease. We may lose our jobs and financial security. We wonder why the Creator has not healed us and returned us to the flyers we once were.

The Potter does not cause the vessel to break. We are clay living in a clay world. The Potter remakes the vessel as seems best to the Potter. That is the promise of God. We will know suffering. We will know spiritual and personal failure. Our lives and the lives of those we love may crumble. We may become new vessels several times in our lives.

Babbie Mason, the gospel singer and songwriter, speaks profoundly in the lyrics of "Trust His Heart." In moments of the journey when you cannot see the plan of God or find the hand of God, she writes, trust God's heart. Sometimes mountains move. Sometimes vessels are broken in the hands of God. There is no clear understanding or explanation. Everything seems as if we are conjuring excuses in an attempt to understand. We trust, sometimes minute by minute, and we ask, "Why?"

Jeremiah writes:

> Blessed are those who trust in the LORD,
>   whose trust is in the LORD.
> They shall be like a tree planted by water,
>   sending out its roots by the stream.
> It shall not fear when heat comes,
>   and its leaves shall stay green;
> in the year of the drought it is not anxious,
>   and it does not cease to bear fruit. (Jeremiah 17:7-8)

Names are important to the historical traditions of Native people. Among some nations or tribes, spiritual names are not spoken except by those who are close relations. To give one's name is to give one's trust, so even today, among some traditional people, children are uncomfortable about giving their names to a stranger. An infant may be given a spiritual name at birth, or the family may wait several years. The spiritual or ceremonial name may reach back into a family's history, or it may reflect a quality the family sees in a child. For example, a child may reflect the character of a grandmother and may be addressed as "Grandmother."

Within the historical structure of Plains tribes is also the tradition of new names or changed names. A person may have a spiritual vision, and his or her name may be changed to reflect that new spiritual responsibility. The community may observe a change in the life or behavior of an individual and begin calling that person by another name. Just as God changed Abraham's name, so too in Native communities can the community change a name by observing changes in behavior, circumstances, or spiritual life.

In the events of our lives, how different would our spiritual communities be if we began calling children by the names of the positive gifts we identify in their character? How might our churches be different if the names we used when we were together described our spiritual vision or growth? Our spiritual names change as our lives change. God is in the business of giving us a new name.

> Abide in me as I abide in you. Just as the branch cannot bear fruit by itself unless it abides in the vine, neither can you unless you abide in me. I am the vine, you are the branches. Those who abide in me and I in them bear much fruit, because apart from me you can do nothing. . . . My Father is glorified by this, that you bear much fruit and become my disciples. (John 15:4-5, 8)

We are not told to bear much fruit; we are asked to abide in the vine. The life from the vine flows through the branches and produces the fruit, and the presence of the fruit is indicative of the vine. When everything around us seems impossible, we are asked to abide in the vine.

After Peter denied Jesus, his world fell into ruin. It wasn't just a perceived spiritual failure; it was a devastation of self-perception and of all that on which he had based his hopes. Imagine facing the remaining ten disciples when what you have believed about yourself appears to have been wrong.

It was Lloyd Ogilvie who wrote that Simon Peter took his denial of Jesus in such a desperate manner because he had assumed that his relationship with Jesus was based on "his capacity to be adequate" (*Ask Him Anything* [New York: Word Books, 1981]).

It was in Peter's moment of deepest inadequacy that God could begin the process of changing his name.

Sometimes lives are broken in the hands of the Potter.

Questions for Discussion and Reflection

1. Think about the story of the death of Dr. C. Everett Koop's son from *Sometimes Mountains Move*. Are there moments when what we believe about God is challenged by what we experience? Explain.

2. What is our understanding of being a *somebody*? How might God define "somebody-ness"?

3. Reflect on / discuss the following thought: "Through the experience of Job we are made aware that good outcomes do not always come from good living."

4. How is it possible that lives can be broken in the hands of the Potter? Reflect on / discuss the difference between being repaired and being made new.

5. Are there moments in your life when you have become aware that your "name has been changed"? What would it mean for you to have a new name through God?

Prayer

Lord of the Dance,
There are no words
to speak suffering.
How do you speak it?
There are no explanations
for the unexplainable.
We are vines, we are clay.
Make us into new vessels.
Keep your hands around us.
Give us new names. Amen.

For Further Reflection

C. Everett Koop and Elizabeth Koop. *Sometimes Mountains Move*. Zondervan, 1995.

Ray Buckley. *The Wing*. Abingdon Press.

Dancing with Holes in Your Moccasins

SCRIPTURE: Read Matthew 5:14; Revelation 21:3.

There was a large circular patch of bare ground in the middle of a field. It had been used so often that the dirt was compacted, packed in on itself. On the surface was fresh dust, as if the earth was shedding her epidermis. Grass rarely grew there, only a few tufts here and there bravely taking a stand. Around the perimeter was a brush-arbor: posts connected on the top by poles, over which had been laid freshly cut boughs. They formed a circle around the area—sentinels providing shade from the sun.

The dance-circle had been swept clean. No one had crossed over it, everyone choosing instead to walk around the circle, as was proper. The crowd had gathered under the arbor, extending far behind it. By the time the drum began to play, the people had been there for a long time. They rose to their feet as an eagle-feather staff was carried into the dance-circle, following the outside of the area. A small group of veterans entered carrying the colors of their country, their feet moving in a step far older than the country itself.

He was the first dancer. Those closest to him could smell the sweet grass and sage on his hair and clothing. From the first step into the sacred circle, his body moved with the drum-song. Every step, once planned and practiced, was second nature to the spirit of the dance. The roach in his hair, made of the guard hairs of porcupine, moved as he turned his head, the tips fanning in precision with the two eagle feathers. Tied to his hips were two outstretched eagle wings forming a bustle, catching the wind from the dance and moving as if still in flight. There was grace in the strength of his dance and exuberance in the control.

Had he not been the first dancer, his footprints may have gone unnoticed. As he danced, moving as the prairie chicken moves, careful steps placed upon the ground, creating the breeze that was caught on the feathers he wore, his feet left marks on the swept earth. There was something different about the footprint, something that made the print recognizable to the other dancers. In the center of each moccasin print, along the ball of the foot, was a large circular impression, worn there by many steps over many years. He was dancing with holes in his moccasins.

Around the circle the dancers moved until they reached the middle and turned outward, the spiral of life moving upon itself and back again. Occasionally, another dancer would acknowledge the first dancer, lifting a dance-fan or touching a piece of dance regalia. It was much more than a greeting. Throughout his life he had noticed a young man who didn't have the resources for something beautiful, and he had spent the winter making something to give him. He would know of an elder with a need and quietly press something into his hands while he passed. To a young woman he would give a beaded knife sheath, or with others drop money at the feet of someone being honored. In gentle, small ways, so as not to seek attention, he would place his gifts in the hands of others, with a nod, saying in effect, "I have made this for you. It is for your dance." Years later, as they passed in other places, they would touch the gifts lightly and keep dancing. "I am wearing your gifts," they seemed to say.

In a tradition of meticulous maintenance of traditional things, the holes were not neglect. They were not signs of carelessness hidden where none could see. The dancer could feel them with every step. Every step brought his foot upon the ground, flesh striking earth. He was reminded of those who could not dance. He was reminded of his people who were unable to dance or who did not have the resources for the materials or a family member with the skill. To dance with holes in his moccasins was a way to remember who he was—a way to remember that dancing was not about beauty or ability but about choosing to dance. Dancing was about stepping out, touching the earth and those around you. Dancing was about giving-away.

Sometimes, gathered around the bed of someone who was ill, my grandmother would sit for hours saying nothing. With her hand resting on the hand of the sick person, or on his or her arm, she would sit quietly while he or she slept, simply touching the person. There was a communication in the silence, an awareness of the other's spirit. She believed in the touch even when there were no words.

This understanding of touching and giving-away is the spiritual stream that flows through many Native cultures. It is what makes us "human beings" not in the sense of humanitarianism but in the sense of living as the Creator intends. To choose to live another way slowly erodes the spirit of our lives until we pull away from God and what God has created. In a real sense, we become alone.

The message of God through Jesus is never-alone-ness. God not only touches us but allows us to touch God. The untouchables are embraced, the outside is brought in, and God chooses to become vulnerable. God gives-away. In the person of Jesus, we see God dancing with holes in God's moccasins. We are not alone, nor can we be. We are meant to dance together.

So many years had passed, and still each year at the annual powwow, thousands of Native people gathered from across the western United States. As the dancers entered the circle, the crowd stood. While snow fell outside, the procession of beautifully attired dancers entered the coliseum. Eagle feathers moved with the dancers. I waited to see him dance, as I did every year in many different places. It was after the Grand Entry, after everyone else danced into the arena, that I saw him.

As in times past, he moved in a clockwise fashion. Every movement of his body was measured and planned, as if he no longer needed to think about it. He had become the dance as one becomes part of a second language you no longer need to translate. He moved his head to the right, as a prairie chicken moves its head. There was the movement to shake the bustles on his arm, and to move the eagle feathers on his head. One could almost hear the bells and see the dance-stick that should have been in his hand. But they weren't there. They were gone.

Over the years he had given the eagle feathers away. The bustles that he once wore in competition had been given to someone else. The bead-work now adorned another dancer. The dance-stick was now carried by another. All of the beautiful adornments were no longer there. His head was ornamented with silver hair. He didn't now enter the arena in com-petition but just to dance. In a starched white shirt, black trousers, and the moccasins with the holes in the bottoms, he danced, having given everything else away. Around the circle in that place, and in many dif-ferent places, others danced, wearing his gifts.

As God enables us, we dance. As God gives to us, we are able to give to others. Because the One who is truly the greatest has become the low-est, we are able to give. We are able to take the gifts of God, not as adorn-ments but as things to be given away. It is grace. Grace to dance, and grace to give-away.

Here is the story of the dancer. It was a shameful thing to break with the tradition. It was the spiritual responsibility of the dancer to maintain both the dance and the regalia he was wearing. If he had dropped an eagle feather, the dance would have come to a halt. Visitors would be asked to put down their cameras. Representative elders would be called, and a ceremony to cleanse the eagle feather would have been prayer-fully conducted. Sometimes the feathers would be taken from the dancer until a respectful amount of time had passed. The dancing was joyful, but it was also accountable to the tradition(s) of those present.

The dancer was dancing with his moccasins in disrepair. His feet were touching the ground through the holes. He was breaking with tradition.

Here is the story of the Lord of the Dance. The ministry of Jesus points us always to God. Jesus touched people whom traditions did not touch. Jesus ate with people whom tradition did not seat at the table. Jesus in-vited those outside of tradition and by so doing acknowledged them as friends in the definition of that tradition. Jesus placed first those who had no status in culture or tradition. But more than that, Jesus did not allow tra-dition to become a measurement on value, treatment of others, or the char-acter of God. Illness was not the result of sin. Poverty was not the result of abandonment by God. Those who are wronged are adopted. Those who do wrong are restored. The betrayer is given the cup of hospitality. Those who had a part in his killing are forgiven before he dies.

It was a Sunday morning in West Africa. During the night, a neighboring church had been bulldozed by soldiers, leaving only a pile of rubble. The people of the church had gathered and worshiped on the rubble. One of the larger churches in the country was farther in the interior and had been built out of wood, like an old tabernacle with a sloping floor and a balcony surrounding the inside. When the worship service began, the building was packed with people filling the doorways and windows. When the congregation was singing, armed soldiers stepped into each doorway and around the windows. Quickly they moved into the balcony and stood. Some began shouting while the people were singing, and although I couldn't understand the words, the intent was clear. The crowd became quiet as people looked around.

The movement was so quiet that at first it wasn't noticeable. An elderly woman moved out of her seat and began slowly walking the aisles of the wooden building with her hands folded in front of her. Her lips were moving as she prayed, the sound barely audible. Another elderly woman stood up and began walking and praying quietly. Another stood, then another. Led by the elderly, one by one people stood up, walking the aisles or standing in place. The individual prayers were not loud, but the crescendo of each added voice filled the church, with only the children looking around. One by one the soldiers left.

This gift of prayer, of the sound of many voices praying at the same time, is also a tradition of prayer. This tradition is the sound of each voice—each person having experienced the grace of God, each heart listening and seeking—joined as one community. Our Korean brothers and sisters bring us this tradition. Sometimes one finds oneself listening to the sound of prayer, as God must, knowing each voice yet experiencing each voice in community. In Oklahoma, our Native communities do the same thing: one voice begins, and others lift up behind it. It is the sound of the wind through leaves. How it must please God!

We are called into community to help each other when it is impossible to dance.

Dance.

Isaiah 49:16 speaks these words: "See, I have inscribed you on the palms of my hands." Literally, I have scratched your life into my skin.

One of the most valued books in my small library is Gerrit Scott Dawson's *Called by a New Name: Becoming What God Has Promised*. After I spoke one day on the Native tradition of giving new names, a friend handed me a copy of the book. In the first chapter of this small book are these words:

> It is pertinent that a Holocaust memorial in Jerusalem bears words from this passage in Hebrew: *yad vashem*, "a monument and a name" (Isaiah 56:5). The memorial declares that meaning will come out of suffering. Those who were slaughtered will be recalled and valued continuously. So they will not be lost. Rather they will become more than what was done to them. Though violence ended their physical lives on earth, the everlasting name from God has continued their presence among future generations ([Nashville: Upper Room, 1997])

"They will become more than what was done to them." You are more than what has been done to you. You are more than what you have done. You are more.

In the tradition of circular story, we find ourselves near the beginning. We are from around the globe. We live in different shelters, eat different foods. We walk different roads. We are so different, yet so alike. We meet, physically or figuratively, and discover that we are wearing the same ashes of Wednesday in hopes of Easter. We are reminded once more of the words of Hans Küng. In all the situations of our lives, in happiness or tears, turmoil or peace, we are "sustained by God, and helpful to men."

Questions for Discussion and Reflection

1. In our time, how do we live while truly giving-away? Is there a difference in giving and living a life of giving-away? Explain your answer.

2. In the story of the dancer, the holes in the moccasins allow his feet to touch the earth. In his life, Jesus taught the disciples humility. Recall

those moments. Are there choices in your faith journey that allow you to do the same?

3. What is the difference between traditions and the gospel? Are there moments when we are compelled to make a choice?

4. Spend some time both alone and with others thinking about how God sustains you and enables you to be helpful to those around you.

Prayer

Lord of the Dance,
Help me to dance,
with holes in my moccasins;
feeling the reality of this life.
Help me to give-away
what has been given to me,
so that others may dance. Amen.

For Further Reflection

Gerrit Scott Dawson. *Called by a New Name: Becoming What God Has Promised.* Nashville: Upper Room, 1997.